The poems in Keeper *ar… d elemental, bracing and embracing. … ng in sudden spiritual moments, work … cCann is a poet of wise, exalting attention: he is a fresh and refreshing new voice in queer poetry.*

Seán Hewitt, author of *Tongues of Fire* and *All Down Darkness Wide*

Mícheál McCann writes some of the most beautiful imagery I have come across in poetry. In Keeper, *we are gifted with McCann's trademark precision of style and form, and offered the deeply reflective lyric in relation to a sensual collectivity; "Where we live our days is as varied as wildflower", where the phrase "Fuck my mouth" transfers itself as tenderly as McCann's speaker to the landscape he inhabits. I was bowled over by the generosity of these poems, felt a physical response towards McCann's poetics of longing, acceptance, and ultimately of safety in* Keeper*'s act of both individual humanity and togetherness; "For just a moment / I'm not at all occupied by where I'm going". These poems are slyly laced with humour and sexuality, beckoning you to wade into them, smiling. The occasion of new work from Mícheál McCann is naturally a cause for celebration, and* Keeper *is exactly that – poems to carry inside you.*

Peter Scalpello, author of *Limbic*

I felt the charm and magic of Keeper, *its gentle enquiry, its tenderness. Felt every line. Full of admiration for Mícheál McCann's quietly life-affirming work.*

Niven Govinden, author of *Diary of a Film*

McCann is a tender, observant rememberer in whose work togetherness tangles with distance. Togetherness wins. From outset to ouch, this gentle, well-wrought book accompanies us through little things; yet has the courage to come face to face with the sudden immensities that stripe the everyday with surreality. A muddy field gasps with eroticism. A father is helpless foreseeing pain he cannot prevent. Sleep is close to death, but also to lovers and neighbours. The wordcraft of these strong, amused, and tender poems will hold you the way an otter holds its favourite pebble to its heart, lying on its furred and musky back, and playing as if the stream of the present were forever, playing hard while loss whisks just around the corner.

Vahni Anthony Capildeo, author of *Like a Tree, Walking*

Keeper

Mícheál McCann

First published in 2022 by Fourteen Publishing.
fourteenpoems.com

Design and typeset by Stromberg Design.
strombergdesign.co.uk

Proofreading and copy editing by Lara Kavanagh.
lk-copy.com

Printed by Print2Demand Ltd, Westoning, Bedfordshire, UK.

ISBN:
978-1-8383943-5-6

for Andrew, with love

If I could I would break into flower
— *Karen Peris*

keeper, n.

- One who or that which keeps or retains, in various senses of the verb. Often *memory.* Also *keeper-back.*
- One who has charge, care, or oversight of any person or thing; a guardian, warden, custodian.
- *Association Football.* A goal-keeper.
- An officer who has the charge of a forest, woods, or grounds, often proudly.
- A simple ring worn in the ears to keep a pierced hole open.

3 a.m.

The day's light had exited without our notice
because we were blocked. The sloe-berry gin
flowed like a long-delayed conversation.

On realising the time and the dark sky
you rose and gasped from an ajar window.
Patches of starling blue signalling tomorrow!

You said, *the sun is rising, thank God*, as though
you had remembered something incredibly important,
and would forget it by the morning.

contents:

Haircut with Beard Trimmer

"And now it seems to me the beautiful uncut hair…"
– Walt Whitman

By halves I do not do things,
so this windowless bathroom becomes
a musky masculine-smelling salon:
towels rolled, toilet rolls stowed,
a starling-blue towel draped over
the thin radiator, warmly, to sculpt
around your neck. You reverse cowboy
the toilet seat and I set to work.
An untrained Brutalist, gently hacking
unsubtle gaps in a burgeoning scalp
where blue veins, like curious dolphins
threaten to approach the surface.
I am the assistant playing games
as the tired master eats some lunch.
And yet to hold a head heavy with duty
whose curls tighten with weariness.
The fuzzy loops of you fall to the tiles
like duck tears, or rain against a window,
muted, as all things are, in those
first few bright moments of wakening.

Romance Option

I direct my avatar in circles and rings
around the desires of a bohemian mage who
addresses me handsomely and hotly as 'thou'
or 'I blush as a stream bleeds red at sunset
seeing your figure appearing in my chambers'.
I hope to impress and make myself necessary,
and just for now I am the only one who knows
that I am pursuing a lithe man, that a world

trembles – uniquely mine – sealed by incantations
and decisions that *will be remembered later*.
The evening birds peep blearily in the loud hedge
of forest flame, and that I play at myself in secret
is no concern to them, and I return to enchanting.
Praise these vessels, rafts to a peopled island.

Keeper

To my memory, I was always on a Gaelic pitch
in autumn, the trees low and big brown mounds
of leaves. A spectrum of brown thrown in the air
by balls skimming the tops like a scalping razor

Relegated to the goalposts – those strong legs –
of the better team, I watch, amazed, as they
run, roll and weave as brave as otters, an owl
watching them play. With my end of the pitch

often vacant and shout-less I would busy myself
with the gravel stones beneath me, articulating
them lovingly into stone palaces around the posts.
I wanted to inhabit each one and feel at home.

My father leans on the side-lines without a cap,
the autumn chill not so unmanageable yet.
His bald head, like the scored ground under
a wooden swing where wildflowers have a chance.

He begins to yell *Mícheál, Mícheál* and not in
disappointment or embarrassment as I thought
immediately, but to pull me from reverie
as the leather ball whirled towards my cheek.

The rasp in his voice not due to my softness,
I learned years later. No, it was how he lay
witness to a great pain careening towards me
through the cold air, and could not catch it.

Just After Rain, 6 p.m.

Waiting things out under the absorbent red
awning of a Pizza Hut, the rain is softly put

and mizzles away to nothing. All the people
walking from work watch it ease from cover

like little sand crabs hiding from seabirds.
I might flower too much and grow so tall!

everyone seems to be saying, given this fear
of being watered in these parts.

The sun stretched its neck for the last time
that day, warming the pavement puddles,

the bowing trees, moist railings; umbrellas
drip glass droplets that feel like newness,

even the rain-spritz from dizzy tires,
throwing misty spray, refracts all rainbow.

I'm nearly home and imagining shakshuka
when the grandeur of a small filling station

catches my eye, or rather the rain falling
from its tin canopy lit by the lowering sun.

Fallen rain falling again. For just a moment
I'm not at all occupied by where I'm going.

Teddy Greets My Mother Who Does Not Flinch

i.m. Jo, i.m. Bo,

That loveless morning where one after the other
they woke early before the passing house martins,

and hobbled out your well-knocked door in search
of one big gulp of air, and the sky, uninterrupted

and so blue; to a cove of familiar seawater,
a horseshoe of a beach in, say Greencastle,

where both dogs are so familiar they do not pause
before throwing their well-brushed legs into water,

and so familiar with this stretch that they assume you
to be observing from the sand. Such is their wisdom.

Despite this, that morning you wake frightened
wondering where they went, and the pain lingers

which is the ultimate comfort, after a fashion,
by which I mean you could not forget them.

Each one its own song, you say over the phone,
just as juvenile scratches sound at your front door.

A new face enters the bright, windowed room,
and pads confidently to the lectern, ready to begin.

He can still smell them, and knows the long smile
you're smiling does not come without great sadness.

Scully

My reports were concise and joyless
before we met. I wear my lab coat
as I begin the first incision of the first
laparotomy of the day's problems.
The skin is ocean-grey. Blood-levels
fine. Alien skin shining like glass.

A classmate in medical school informs
me I'll never be lonely knowing everything.
Making sense of all this pain with facts
and straight faces is my way of praying.
Eventually my sceptical eyes counting
drug levels or bullets in a peashooter

grow wide to mystery. At the end of
each day like each episode I remember
how I am a grain of sand in a twelve-
year-old terrarium; an unresolved
anatomical question, or the reflection
of myself cast in your believing eyes.

Confirming What We Knew

We are lying together quietly as the night becomes morning
when you ask me where I look for 'beauty'

(You hunch two fingers into a wrinkled rabbit to make
your sardonicism clear. An elfish smile in the dark.)

and I think your pleased sigh meant there was a simple answer
that sailed over my head while I sank into cartoon thought.

Consider a six-and-a-half-foot lad with thighs as tight as harp strings,
with a chest so firm, a rolling terrain to lollop down,

and then the long train carriage of a penis, intimidating
and decontextualised, like a beech branch, lying on the path;

and then the sorry yard just resting underneath this window
(my heart) that belches butterburs, nasturtiums, coltsfoot.

No difference, I eventually reply, in the GAA fella and the wine-fade
shade of those weeds that clamber through that gravel outside.

You pause. And what when the coffee cup is empty, I say,
and stained along the blue enamel's rim? Will beauty know

how the twitch of my eye means *here we go…* or that I am
at my saddest with all those glittering people around me?

Heaven is a garden, you say, and while roasting fragrant beans
I think, And what about all that time between now and then?

The Ambulance Driver

Now you are dead, how do you
expect me to stop straining to see
through the tinted windscreens
of each one that passes by?

Some go slowly, others charge.
One pulls up beside me at the red light
I always seem to find myself at.
Her eyes catch mine, desperate,

and I'll think you're trying to
tell me something important,
but the light's gone green, and
she's gone before I could ask.

Two bin liners of his shoes

after Leontia Flynn

Two bin liners of his shoes
are hauled from the car boot
and carried up one stair flight;
the coal black sacks strain

and fray grey at tear-points
where the thirty shoes in each
burden them beyond their means.
They find fraying carpet just in time.

The bricks of the houses
of the city are exhaling into
the unexpected heat of a May day
in a memorably cold spring

(the trees are only finding
their hairs again), and these bags
spew out boots and trainers
that I pair and pair and touch a while.

Not odour but fragrance greets me
in my sorting: the heady bath
of a man's house, not a man's
feet… I recognise their smell

as though the former owner
was leaning back in the dark corners
of the well-sun-lit room. A duo
of flat shoe Docs tap their way to me

like little baristas I find attractive,
and I brush the dust from them
(which feels like a violence)
and then slip them on. Bit tight,

ouch, I say at the outset
of a long walk that becomes
a long sit on a fishing stand
by the Lagan so glassy and inviting

another world beneath, and then
here come the bougie rowers to ruin it.
So I sit in a man's shoes
he never had the day to break in

and observe with Biblical detachment
my blood form a small diamond
in sock fabric like a gift
and wonder if I am making the dead laugh.

I rise unsteadily to my full height,
unsure how I'll manage
that short walk home. I never realise
daffodils are going, only them gone.

John 20:15

Had I personally returned from death
corporeal, raging, I could have run
to find my shivering wispish lover,
if not dressing my naked form first
in limp rags or bevelled palm fronds.

Yet he stayed by the yawning mouth
of his tomb, so the story goes, pruning
fuchsia or cotton thistles. Why else
would he be mistaken for a gardener?
Here the dead tend their graves for visitors.

Were it that we inhabited our bodies newly
each morning, and then could recognise
our last day simply: soil clumps falling
from our fingers as we turn to face
the woman calling and calling our name.

Big City Types

Now we'll certainly be stopping
cultchie-this and *plaid-shirt-shone-*
brown-shoes-that, indeed; and less
of your lamenting us poor folks'
long days under wakening
and path-clearing rains.
Don't you worry heavy-bagged traveller,
we'll manage. And let's agree
to never again recall your idea
that those who stay here in this city,
run through by a windingly grey and bracing river,
are engaged in a constant political act.

Where we live our days is as varied as wildflower,
blooming steadily or shifting colour and place.
Don't feel bad for those
who are not seduced by heat or change,
they have their own, blessed concerns.
Anchors are only found in the sea.
Come along now, a plane is planning
to take you away from here,
and the rain will still fall, and the days persist
varied and expansive as an orrery,
or the shadows of people on often
rebuilt, well-walked walls.

Keep chasing the sun long enough
and you'll meet your shadow coming back.

Late Blight

The field had spent years drinking
rain and pills, received infusions, dialysis,
pesticide repair. Now Creeslough breathes again.
Its scarred mouth opens, sleep furry.
The field is threaded through for the new
harvest, overwintered. The lambs
heartily woollen, bounce over orange soil
to find a newer water, frost-hardy.
Some are quick-footed. Some come back later,
others love this image: their children alive;
young ones loving cappuccinos. The field
understood, knew they had to flock elsewhere,
busy re-stitching its root intestine networks.

Years later the field, mid-Rosary, was appeared to.
Two boys in soil-brown dungarees, one leading
the other by the hand. Not disturbing
the braided potato ridges, they skirt the edges
and disappear into a thin wood. *Fuck*
my mouth hears the field, and in response
hopes they stay. It has pierced its ears
with helleborine and blue-eyed grass.
The boys come out eventually
from the trees holding cans like prayer beads.
Come back home says the field.
Some beer is spilled generously for the field.
I'm awake! the field says, reeling.

Surreal

This particular Monday feels like a moon-sized citrus,
and frustrated turbots are standing in for the night stars.

The lowly-burned candle loses inhibition and rigidness,
a figurative candle in the wind, it vomits a river of wax!

A black cat pins a glossy red umbrella underneath
its right armpit; curses the rain; greets me tersely.

The morning walk is waylaid by all the brown leaves
littered on the river's tabletop, outgoing correspondence.

On those days where an alarm is eschewed yet
the gold of the morning still seems kind, and for you.

The feline, under its other armpit, drops ten books
into a violently blue puddle. *My Proust!* He hisses!

Sometimes I feel like the only way I can describe you
is through these dream places I find, temples regreened.

Often, early, crocuses bang their heads, being only young.
If this doesn't offer you sense don't be discouraged.

These are but the things I see. The very firmament
of things which shimmer and baulk strangely, reassuring me.

Marginalia

In 1907 the 374 jewels that composed the Irish Crown Jewels went missing from Dublin Castle while under the supposed protection of Arthur Vicars, the Ulster King of Arms. A subsequent Scotland Yard investigation uncovered a coterie of homosexuals resident within Dublin Castle, and the investigation was halted. Francis Shackleton, Vicars' "housemate" for two years, was one of the prime suspects, but left Ireland shortly after and fell into obscurity. Some years later, stripped of his rank and reputation, Vicars was pulled from his home by a local IRA regiment and forced to watch his house burn down, then was shot. The Scotland Yard report was "lost", and the jewels were never found.

Oh Francis,

I haven't much time to say what things
occur to me now. Worse this letter
may never reach you; what address
could you keep now your heart's sent
you fleeing, when could you stop running?
If the most we may say is in hint then
let us recall in wanton euphemism
how *decent, if eccentric* men
like us happened across one another,
shared one cigarette under a lamplight,
or in the shadow of the Albert Clock,
knocked a little bit *about the town*,
partook in several midnight suppers.
Frank, if I had one minute more on this
bursting world I would take it entirely
in those precious, shaded dalliances.
I am brought to my knees now by men
who have provoked Kilmorna into flame;
they want me to watch the house
char and collapse but little do they appreciate
I was born onto marshy, boggy ground,
unsteady terrain ahead of me always,
and will die on it now…

I was never truly at ease in Bedford Tower
or sheltering beneath those stone columns
for a smoke as men passed with attaché cases.
They could never imagine those parties.
Allow me this last peace of imagination:
you on the back of a deep-brown horse,
trotting towards Ulster. The sky is clear.
The Order of Saint Patrick, pilfered,
clings to your skin underneath a thread-vest,
dressing a sleekit neck that is well-warmed
by some man's attention. May it persist
that pulse in your throat, and those jewels
disturbed slightly with each throb of you.
My home is a window into flame; embers leap
upwards from the fire like orange butterflies,
and in the eyes of the man in front of me
I see glimmers of my fast-ruining home, yes,
but imagine them to be those jewels I lost.
A final gift of sorts, you might say. Imp!
Throwing your head back, gallivanting.
The fire is laughing heartily with you…
I hope your journey north or seaward
is short and peaceful, but I suspect
it has barely begun. 'Horizon' is a word
that means too much to men like us.
Thrust on toward it Frank, and sometime
you'll land on a rain-softened, kinder soil.
If you ever return to this glade visit me.
I'll be near some prayer of running water.

Bless you, bless your whole life.

A.

Pea Risotto on Tuesday, Lemony Salmon with Couscous on Wednesday

for Nigella Lawson, with gratitude

A mustard footstool holds me up,
brought kitchen-way especially
so to witness this flour-crowned
dough, for the side, *transforming*.

The difference in fragrance from
a verdant pepper to its bumblebee sibling;
a mind is only rolling meatballs as
it rolls meatballs, humming away.

After the day, or the year, that was
in it, my frame sags with weary,
and yet I look into this scarlet pepper
as though it were a zipline to peace.

Little cherry tomato eyeballs halve
and *spritz jubilantly* in themselves.
I stir, fold and enrich the risotto,
prayerlike, despite a hungry face

resting on my left shoulder. Salt flakes
to taste. Some more just because
it tastes rounder. I'm trying to say
you remind us to be kind, it saved me.

Immanence

A raspberry one with moist frosting, or
a lemon one with white chocolate shavings?
A door chime signals us. A donut for two in
a café with notions on a sleepy Lisburn Road.
The low buzz chat of other people engaged
in another try. Exposed soft white light bulbs
make everything rounder. Do you see them?
Some good coffee. Two brightly green eyes.

Hammers of wet coffee grounds into the bin
remind us we're here; our treasure is delivered.
What we have been waiting for all this time.
Slowly, a dull blade halves the red-glaze donut
and it cries laughing. Blood is coming out!
You're wearing my jumper. You're eating.

Tense

Kneeling onto soft earth, greedy from
the rainfall, I struggle to pinpoint
when the person underfoot evanesced
out of living anecdote and story into that
tense which holds death by the collar.

While the magpies thrust from *here*
to *were here*, and our shoulders
go from dry to burdened, you have been
quietly travelling to the past tense, and
no one noticed, until you had arrived there.

Something I Believe

For a few of our shared seconds
my forehead rests along
the shield of your shoulder
as I hunt for
a reticent seat belt.

Languoring here against wool,
against green-grey stripes,
my vision blackens as I grope
for a handhold. Lacoste,
and the Lagan following the car.

That it comforted me,
this amateur embrace,
that you caught my eye briefly
then turned to your nephew,
the road ongoing, the water untroubled.

Seemingly cursory,
certainly to your family,
maybe even you.
A thieved intimacy,
a night in a balmy harbour.

This is our inheritance:
a music that recalls flowing water
for those without the ears to hear
all the tiny water creatures living
underneath, quartz in our gills.

Aubade with Bombay Cat

Reluctantly woken by the rattles of magpies
outside the square window, I fume and plot

and go to feed the young cat with shiny fur.
Then a 2-cup percolator fills with water, grounds

compacted and set onto severe heat. The day
still boasts a certain quiet at this early point,

the only noise being the lessening trees swaying.
It has been a difficult winter. Two espresso cups

fill with fragrant espresso like coinage.
You receive your doubloon with reluctant

consciousness, and every day I encounter
you or you encounter me like this: heady

with sleep, stranger-like when rousing;
every morning like the first, you seem distant

and alluring, as I hand you this clay cup
for the first time, and then again, then again.

Lying, half-talking in bed, Giles struggles
onto the yellow floral bedspread, juvenile

and klutzy, lowering into the rivulet, the canyon
made by our feet and legs under the duvet

with an inscrutable and handsome face.
Two men lying before him, mostly quiet

and he doesn't seem so perturbed. He even
ignores the pair of magpies that gaze in

through the veil of the morning at us three
laying top-to-toe; an intimidating trio…

The room dressed in a muted a.m. light.
You proffer yourself as a palatial pillow.

I joke, ask if the reason he bites so much
is because he's confused, needs a mother figure

and before you answer he catches a toe
between two incisors so faithfully

that I proclaim my faith in the virgin birth
and my chest erupts into a river of coffee.

The kind woman upstairs probably wakes
thinking we have discovered a new *avenue*

or that this elegant cat is an egalitarian at heart.
In soreness I gently lift the librarian up

and shut him out of the bedroom. You redden
in the effort not to laugh, relinquishing eventually,

and Giles peals a few squeaks on the other side.
As the sharpness of pain fades, I grow penitent

and like all the loves I have left in my life,
eventually go to peer through this keyhole

to find nothing but darkness on the other side.
When I come to and ease open the heavy door

the small teacup of a cat is gone. Now alone
(you doze, love) I begin looking for him.

Song

The quiet roll of the drum
of the washing machine,
some residual heat giving
from the long radiator
against my backside.
How a rose opens more
and more as it dies, wanting
to share one more thing.
To think I once volunteered
to eschew all this music.
The washing machine roars
through the thick walls
as the first day of winter
poses like a dusty photograph
you blow on. The motes lift off,
smile-inducing. I persist
regardless, against all advice.

Envoi

These empty and agonised nights
you retire early; I sit up for matins.
The light and you rise secretly, while
the evening still shades my eyelids.

As I reluctantly take to the outdoors,
even the premature daffodils bow
their papery, lowered shoulders.
Daylight leaves gloom in no doubt.

Instead, night and I have hooked up,
bosom-buddies, collegial hecklers,
but most often we listen. A small-
sounding dog bark. Coming wind.

The appropriate hush of this time
and just the light of one small lamp
throws our tat into dramatic focus.
Lamplight pierces through Murano

glass octopi: one navy, one orange,
sea glass colours. The cat throned
on an iron trivet. A post-it on a door
reads *Prayer to Obtain Divine Love.*

If I pretend, I can hear the calm tide
of your breath these few rooms over
as reassuring as a dog heart or stone
when I really hear a colossal quiet.

Struck by the slantness of your things
all cast dark, and you deeply asleep,
a Babylonian translation exercise
poses itself to recall each circumstance.

A photo, a candleholder, a favourite mint.
The unkind night continues questioning
and I imagine you absconded for good,
so that you cannot easily trouble me.

I spend the rest of tonight's lateness
wishing I were brave enough to pull you
back into life, encourage us outside
where the soft mizzle, where the moon.

Notes and Acknowledgements

I would like to thank the editors of the following publications for publishing some of these poems: *The Poetry Review, Queering the Green, fourteen poems, The Manchester Review, Poetry Ireland Review,* and *bath magg.* "Marginalia" was commissioned as part of the MAC's NINOW100 program.

"Romance Option" is named after a term within video gaming that outlines certain non-playable characters that the player can romance over the course of the game.
"Scully" is in the voice of Dana Scully à la *The X Files*.
"Late Blight" refers to the fungus, a water mould, that resulted in the Irish potato famine from 1845 to 1849.
"Marginalia" owes its cadence to Sinéad Morrissey's poem "Vanity Fair".
"John 20:15" echoes a line from "The Boy" by Marie Howe.
"Immanence" is the theological antonym of transcendence. In other words, a theory that the divine manifests in every singular aspect of the material world, even patisserie items.

I'm grateful and indebted to Charles Lang, Kelly O'Brien, Ellen Orchard, Nidhi Zak/Aria Eipe, and Eva Griffin for so many conversations, as well as with Leontia Flynn, Stephen Sexton, and Gail McConnell. I had the fortune to work with Colette Bryce on some of these poems, and her encouragement and example has been very formative.

I'm knee-bendingly thankful to have the opportunity to work with Ben Townley-Canning as my editor, for the long conversations and warm support of the poems. To have an editor with such a broad and encompassing hope for poetry is a gift.

All the love poems are for Andrew Cunning (and newly Giles); the elegies for Desmond Wilson. "Romance Option" is for Eva Griffin; "Keeper" for my father; "Song" for my remarkable brother.

Thanks to my friends and family, how blended the two have become.